HOW TO PREVENT PASSIVE-AGGRESSIVE PEOPLE FROM WREAKING HAVOC USING SCIENCE

A Humanist Learning Systems Companion Book

By Jennifer Hancock

I0402596

Published by Jennifer Hancock

Copyright 2019 by Jennifer Hancock

Published 2019

Paperback Edition

ISBN: 9781798643426

Imprint: Independently published

Title: How To Prevent Passive-Aggressive People from Wreaking Havoc Using Science

Author: Jennifer Hancock

Editor: Desiree Vogelpohl

This book is also available as an ebook or audio book at most online retailers

Table of Contents

CHAPTER 1: INTRODUCTION 7

CHAPTER 2: PASSIVE-AGGRESSIVE BEHAVIOR DEFINED 11

CHAPTER 3: WHY PEOPLE BEHAVE PASSIVE-AGGRESSIVELY.. 13

CHAPTER 4: EXAMPLES 19

CHAPTER 5: WHY IT NEEDS TO BE DEALT WITH 25

CHAPTER 6: BEHAVIORAL SCIENCE ON HOW BEHAVIORS ARE
LEARNED AND UNLEARNED 27

CHAPTER 7: HOW TO REMOVE REWARDS FOR A PASSIVE-
AGGRESSIVE PERSON 33

CHAPTER 8: YOUR GOAL 39

CHAPTER 9: ABOUT THE AUTHOR 41

CHAPTER 1: INTRODUCTION

Hi – my name is Jennifer Hancock and this is how to prevent passive-aggressive people from wreaking havoc in the workplace using science.

I normally teach how to stop bullying and harassment using behavioral science techniques, but in every presentation I do, I get questions on how to deal with passive-aggressive behavior. Which is one of the many ways bullying and harassment manifests in the workplace. To me, passive- aggressive people are so predictable and so easy to manipulate that it doesn't cross my mind to address this problem specifically, but there is nothing so obvious as what isn't obvious and this is the case with passive-aggressive behavior.

This book discusses how passive-aggressive behavior is rewarded. Techniques to ensure passive- aggressive behavior doesn't interfere with workflow, how to take responsibility for your part of the interaction, and how to make sure you aren't part of the problem. This discussion will cover three reasons why people behave passive-aggressively and help you learn how to respond professionally and effectively to the problem so that these individuals don't wreak havoc in your workplace.

Learning Objectives

1) Learn a science-based approach to dealing with passive-aggressive employees

2) Understand how compassion and professionalism can help resolve workplace behavior issues

3) Be able to reinforce organizational core values by modeling respectful behavior in difficult situations

Topics Covered
- Why people behave passive-aggressively
- When it's not passive-aggressive but a symptom of something else
- How to manage a truly passive-aggressive situation using behavioral science

Note:
This is the companion book to the online course 'How to Prevent Passive-Aggressive People from Wreaking Havoc Using Science.' This book contains transcripts of the course for easy home reference.

Individuals and groups can benefit from this course. For more information on this course visit https://humanistlearning.com/passiveaggressivepeopl e/

Overview: Science & Philosophy

This book is going to combine science and philosophy, specifically behavioral science and humanistic philosophy. Behavioral science will help us understand why passive-aggressive people are behaving the way they do, how they are rewarded, and how we can use this information to neutralize their worst tendencies. Humanistic philosophy is going to help us think about the situation differently through a compassionate lens – and this in turn is going to help us actually implement the strategy behavioral science says we should use.

According to science, the best way to neutralize the negative impacts of a passive-aggressive person – is by being compassionate, nice, and professional. Isn't it great that science validates taking a compassionate humanistic approach? It means – living your values will help you be successful when dealing with problematic people.

~~~~~

CHAPTER 2: PASSIVE-AGGRESSIVE BEHAVIOR DEFINED

Wikipedia has this to say about passive-aggressive behavior: "In psychology, passive-aggressive behavior is characterized by a habitual pattern of non-active resistance to expected work requirements, opposition, sullenness, stubbornness, and negative attitudes in response to requirements for normal performance levels expected. Most frequently it occurs in the workplace, where resistance is exhibited by indirect behaviors such as procrastination, forgetfulness, and purposeful inefficiency, especially in reaction to demands by authority figures, but it can also occur in interpersonal contexts." - https://en.wikipedia.org/wiki/Passive%E2%80%93aggressive_behavior

The hallmark is that the person is resisting or being aggressive by not doing something. They may just not do the work requested. Or they may withhold information. Or they may not invite a certain person to an important meeting – or "forget" to include them in an email. All of these behaviors may be innocent mistakes. Or… they could be active acts of resistance or worse, sabotage. That's why this is considered a passive form of aggression. They are acting out by omission, by not doing something.

So what is going on? Well, it depends on the individual and their motivations – if they have any. Not doing something is a way to control what is going on. As an act of resistance, it is quite powerful. Some people may be resisting because they don't like what is going on and are using one of the only tools at their disposal – non-compliance.

In general, most managers are adept at handling this sort of situation and wouldn't really consider it a severe case. In fact, when I asked about this, a friend of mine admitted to doing things like this and I had to laugh because he clearly has never dealt with a truly passive-aggressive person. He was merely showing up at a workshop he found boring and was using the time to grade papers instead.

To me, passive-aggressive behavior is when entire work flows come grinding to a halt because of one person. Or when entire departments have to work around one person just to get things done. Or when one person is actively sabotaging the work of other members of the community by withholding needed resources.

Passive-aggressive behavior is a tool of social control, which is why it's considered a possible manifestation of bullying or harassment. If someone has the power to prevent another person from getting their work done, they have the power to bully or harass that person.

~~~~~

CHAPTER 3: WHY PEOPLE BEHAVE PASSIVE-AGGRESSIVELY

There are several reasons why people might behave in a passive-aggressive way.

Frustration

They may be frustrated or angry and do not have the ability or authority to voice objections, so they object by complying but not complying, like my friend does when forced to attend workshops he isn't interested in. He is exerting control over a situation he has no control over.

Strategic

Another reason someone might behave passive-aggressively is they are being strategic.

There is long history of passive aggression as resistance, actually. Passive-aggressive behavior is probably one of the few tools of resistance an enslaved person can use to resist without being killed. Creative and strategic ways to resist enslavement would be – to slow down your work and not be efficient. Maybe break the tools accidentally so you can't work. Pretend to not understand the instructions. Pretend to be too sick to work. Passive-aggressive behavior isn't always bad. It may be a form of legitimate resistance.

There are a few things I want you to understand about this. First, the next time you perceive a worker to be lazy, you may want to question why. Perhaps the problem isn't that they are being lazy. Maybe there is something else going on and they are resisting.

Also, if you ever hear the generalization that black people are lazy – understand that they aren't. That stereotype is a result of their active resistance to enslavement. And yes, this still needs to be said because the biases that arose as a result of enslavement are still with us today and are still impacting dynamics in the workplace. So check your assumptions and find out what is really going on and why, and approach these situations with compassion.

BULLYING AS STRATEGIC PASSIVE AGGRESSION
Another way this behavior may be strategic is because, ultimately, this behavior is about exerting control in a way so you can hide what you are doing. Which is why some bullies use this technique, too. Instead of using this behavior to resist oppression, the behavior is used to oppress through active sabotage of the workflow. A bully can use the techniques to target an individual to make their work harder to do. It is no longer about an individual resisting work. It is now about preventing someone else from getting their work done.

Most of the time, when I get asked about passive-aggressive behavior in the workplace, it falls into this category. Someone "forgets" to invite someone to a meeting or doesn't include them in planning for something that impacts their area of expertise. Or they withhold resources.

I used to work in an office with a passive-aggressive person. She and I were both directors in charge of different departments. She would ask me for help, but not provide me with the resources I needed to do the work for her, then she would complain that I wasn't being helpful or that my delays, caused by her inactions, were causing her to not get her work done.

Sound familiar? I'm sure you all have experienced something like this at some point.

The person doing this is specifically targeting an individual to make their work and life harder. It is not uncommon for harassment and discrimination to take this form so that the aggressor has plausible deniability. They forgot. Or they sent it and what do you mean you didn't get it? They ghost and claim they didn't know. The point is, by being passive-aggressive they can find excuses for their behavior and can get away with actively sabotaging the work of someone else.

Pathological

Another way this might happen is if the person is behaving this way pathologically – meaning – it is not being done strategically. The person doing this just isn't in control of their behavior enough to do this well. People who behave this way with everyone are doing it pathologically. They gum up the works for everyone. They are probably the most annoying because they are the most obvious. Everyone on the team is affected by them so everyone is aware of the problem and wants it fixed.

The problem is – if someone is not being strategic, but pathological – it's not fixable. They are not in control enough of their behavior to hide what they are doing.

I am not a psychologist and won't be giving you advice on how to handle someone with a real mental health problem. All you can do when someone is doing this pathologically is understand it's not going to get better and the person in question should be treated with compassion as they are most likely dealing with a mental health issue. You will always have to work around them and if your company has the resources to do that – great. If they don't, you should get rid of them.

The Real Danger

The real danger is the people who are behaving passively aggressive to strategically bully, harass, or sabotage an individual. While the strategic bully is hurting workflow, they are really only targeting a couple of people, so the people not targeted aren't experiencing it. What is happening, when strategic, may very well look like an interpersonal conflict.

When someone does this pathologically, everyone knows it. When someone does this strategically, as a way to dominate or harass someone, it can be very hard to see. But it is no less damaging to the organization and the workflow.

Which brings me back to passive-aggressive behavior as a tool of resistance. If someone isn't getting their work done, are they being lazy? Are they incompetent? Are they resisting something? Or are they being sabotaged?

At first glance, it is impossible to know. Fixing the problem depends on diagnosing it properly. You can't always rely on managers to report what is happening properly because it isn't unusual for managers to bully and harass staff and to sabotage an employee they don't like.

Things that look passive-aggressive might not be and you might be misreading what is happening entirely.

~~~~~

CHAPTER 4: EXAMPLES

An Example of Strategic Passive-Aggressive Behavior

At my very first job at an ice cream parlor, I was hired by the owner but the manager was upset about it. The manager scheduled me at times I couldn't work and then just didn't put me on the schedule at all. I wasn't a bad person, the manager used her power to make me fail. She did it in a way that held her blameless.

She used what power she did have to control a situation that was beyond her control, and she did it successfully. I'm sure she accused me of not being a good employee because I couldn't meet her demands, which would have required me to ditch high school to work.

An Example of Pathological Passive-Aggressive Behavior

Let me give you an example of someone who was pathologically passive-aggressive, meaning she did this with everyone.

I used to work at a non-profit in Los Angeles. I was the director of volunteer services, the pathologically passive-aggressive individual was the director of fundraising. One time she organized a fundraising event. I didn't know until we got there that it was a volunteer appreciation dinner because I was never told that was what this was. I was not consulted on who the volunteers were and who might be worthy of an award. I was not asked for addresses to send out invites to the volunteers receiving the awards. Nothing. I had no idea this event had anything to do with volunteers until I got there.

Let this sink in: the director of volunteer services was excluded from planning on an event to honor volunteers. It sounds crazy – and it was. This really happened. I'm not making this up. I showed up to what I thought was a normal fundraising dinner to find that it was a volunteer awards dinner, with no volunteers in attendance. Seriously. None. Imagine an academy awards event and none of the winners are present. None. That was what this was like.

The executive director didn't know it was a volunteer awards dinner. The board of directors didn't know it was a volunteer awards dinner. The only people who knew it was a volunteer awards dinner was this woman and her assistant.

After it became apparent that this was an awards dinner that had failed to invite the awardees to the dinner, the president of the board and the rest of the members of the board started openly laughing at the surreal spectacle we were witnessing. Because it wasn't like they gave out one award. They gave out almost 20 awards to people who weren't there. No one who got an award was there. No one!!!!

Why did she do something this ridiculously stupid? My guess is she did this to make me look bad. She did this sort of thing all the time. She would withhold information from me and then kept trying to blame me for things not getting done. Obviously, what she did in this case backfired on her because she was caught. But she was caught all the time, because she did this to everyone. All the time. Which is why the board of directors wanted nothing to do with her and were openly mocking her at the event.

I was friends with one of her assistants who once confided in me that she was upset because she knew another department needed information but that her boss had forbidden her to give it to them. How insane is that? Pretty insane. I'd like to think she was being passive-aggressive to strategically hide her incompetence. But really, it was her passive-aggressive behavior that MADE her incompetent.

Putting a number on the cost of passive-aggressive behavior
How much damage did she cause in a 5-year period before they were able to fire her? She burned through a $10 million-dollar endowment because she was so incredibly bad at her job. Because instead of doing her job, she spent her time trying to figure out how to make others look bad.

Strategic Passive-Aggressive Behavior as Harassment and Discrimination

My final example has to do with discrimination. I have a friend who works in construction and her company has a really hard time keeping black employees. According to her, they just aren't as productive as they need them to be. She came to me asking for help on how to train the black employees to be more productive. My friend was making erroneous assumptions about WHY these employees were not working to their potential. She thought maybe they just didn't have a good work ethic.

The real reason these employees were not as productive as their other "white" employees has to do with active discrimination in the form of passive-aggressive behavior from their clients AND their vendors AND their coworkers. Withholding information, slowing down and not responding in a timely manner, and giving bad information intentionally are passive-aggressive acts of sabotage.

A white employee in the same job may never experience this sort of problem and so it might never occur to them that another individual may appear to be less productive because their ability to get the job done is being actively sabotaged by bigots.

This happens to women too, by the way. What's the old saying – you have to work twice as hard to be considered half as good? It's true if you are being victimized by active passive-aggressive sabotage, which has wide-ranging effects throughout our society.

If you are looking to create diverse but cohesive workgroups, you need to take this seriously. When you are looking at a workflow problem, it is impossible to know at first glance whether the person not getting the work done is being lazy, or whether they are incompetent, or whether they are passive-aggressively resisting something. Or whether they are being victimized by passive- aggressive sabotage. You can't know this, so don't make assumptions.

~~~~~

CHAPTER 5: WHY IT NEEDS TO BE DEALT WITH

For obvious reasons, having a member of the team that is actively sabotaging the work is a bad thing. I'm pretty sure no one hires people to not get their work done. Yet, we seem to just – accept passive-aggressive behavior in the workplace as a given. It's not a given and it should not be tolerated.

This problem is also one of the many reasons why workplace diversity initiatives fail. Passive-aggressive behavior can and is used to target marginalized people to prevent them from being successful and as a way to harass them, all while making them look bad.

The final reason passive-aggressive behavior needs to be dealt with is because it prohibits good problem-solving. Good problem-solving is collaborative. It is based on accurate information. It is geared towards finding the best ideal solution. While ideal solutions aren't always available, good problem-solving should at least be the goal of everyone on the team.

Since the main method of passive-aggressive individuals is sabotage, what they are aiming for is for no solution. You can't collaboratively solve a problem when one of the team member's goal is to make sure the problem isn't solved. You also can't make good decisions when someone is withholding critical information about the problem. You also can't solve the problem, even if there is agreement, if someone is withholding the resources needed to solve the problem.

Do you see where I am going with this?

Passive-aggressive people wreak havoc in the workplace because they prevent problems from being solved. When problems don't get solved, they fester. You end up with unhappy employees and unhappy customers. If that persists, you eventually won't have a business. Because businesses, all businesses, are in the business of solving problems.

Whether your business is feeding people, cleaning rooms, or environmental remediation. All businesses are in the business of solving problems. Anything that prevents good problem-solving is detrimental to your business. It also harms morale and makes your customers cranky. If it turns out this behavior is being directed at someone in a protected class as a way to harass or discriminate against them, you could also end up with EEO lawsuits.

We need to deal with this for personal reasons, professional reasons, and for ethical reasons.

~~~~~

CHAPTER 6: BEHAVIORAL SCIENCE ON HOW BEHAVIORS ARE LEARNED AND UNLEARNED

Now that we understand more about what this behavior is and why it happens, let's talk about how to make it stop.

All behavior is learned. If you have a behavior that is happening, it's being rewarded. Even if it seems completely counterintuitive to do it, like the fundraising director who was making herself look like an idiot out of her pathological need to make others look bad. Her behavior was rewarded at some point. Often, it is rewarded immediately.

If your goal is to make others suffer, withholding is a great way to do that, and you get an immediate reward. Especially if this is done strategically as a form of bullying, harassment, or discrimination. If the boss can't see the reason why the person you don't like isn't getting their work done, you can get them fired. That's a pretty hefty reward at very low cost.

I'm not going to go too deeply into the behavioral science of how behaviors are rewarded and extinguished, except to give you the highlights of the findings.

There are 3 main things you need to understand if you want to get unwanted behavior to stop.

1) What are reinforcements.

2) Why and how behaviors are rewarded and how to change the rewards and cost.

3) Reinforcement schedules.

I'm going to give a quick overview of the science and then we will discuss how exactly to apply it to passive-aggressive people.

Reinforcements

First – reinforcements. There are 3 types of reinforcements. Positive – where the person likes what happens. Negative or punishment – where they don't. And neutral – which is neither good nor bad.

According to 7 plus decades of research on how to stop unwanted behaviors, the way to get a behavior to stop is to stop rewarding it. That seems obvious, but in real life removing rewards is rather hard. Which is why most people – when they want to stop an unwanted behavior – tend to punish or go negative. The problem is that the effects of negative or punishment are mixed and often counterproductive.

THE PROBLEM WITH PUNISHMENT
Basically, negative reinforcement or punishment only really works on first exposure, meaning the first time the behavior occurs. After that, it tends to strengthen the unwanted behavior instead of extinguishing it. For example:

The first time I ate a hot dog, I got sick and threw up. I literally have never eaten a hot dog since. The smell of them makes me nauseous. This is the power of negative reinforcement on a first or early learning experience. The individual associates the negative experience with the stimulus - in this case a hot dog - and avoids it. But this only works when the behavior is new.

When the behavior is established, meaning it's been positively rewarded for a while, negative reinforcement has the opposite effect. It strengthens the behavior instead of extinguishing it.

I spent a summer in China on an exchange trip when I was in college. During this trip, everyone on the trip became obsessed with ice cream. Why? Because we kept getting really crappy ice cream. But every once in a while, we got really good ice cream there. The effect of having bad ice cream did not make us never want to have ice cream again, because we knew, we could get good ice cream. Our love of ice cream was already established. The bad experiences we had, made us want ice cream more, not less. This is exactly what is predicted by the science. Negative reinforcement of established behaviors, strengthens the behavior.

How to remove the reward for unwanted behavior

It is safe to assume that in the workplace, if you are seeing a behavior, it is not the first time the behavior has occurred. It is probably an established behavior pattern and that punishment not only won't work, it will make things worse.

Since we don't want to positively reward a behavior, and because punishment is probably going to strengthen the behavior we don't want, that leaves our only option – neutral response. This is done by removing the reward. There are a variety of ways to do that with passive-aggressive people, which we will get into in the next chapter. For now, what I want you to understand is that 70 plus years of research have shown that the most effective way to stop unwanted behavior is to remove the reward via neutral response.

Reinforcement Schedules

There is one last thing you need to be aware of and that is reinforcement schedules. Basically, how often does the person get a particular type of response.

There are two possible reinforcement schedules: consistent and variable. Consistent is when they get the same type of reinforcement every time. Variable is when they get different responses.

According to the research, the most effective schedule for behavioral extinction is consistent. Variable reinforcement actually escalates the behavior and makes it worse. Consistent will get it to stop. Not right away. The individual will "fight" back and there is a whole lot of science as to why that is. Just know that resistance to removal of reward is predicted to occur, but that if you consistently remove the reward, eventually they will stop. If you variably remove the reward, they not only won't stop, they will get progressively worse.

FOR EXAMPLE:
The reason my friends and I were obsessive about ice cream in China was because sometimes we got good ice cream and sometimes we got bad ice cream. The variable nature of the reinforcements we were receiving caused us to obsessively seek out the reward of good ice cream. The existence of bad ice cream, not only didn't deter us, it made our obsession worse. If we had consistently had bad ice cream, we would have stopped looking for it. If we had consistently good ice cream, we would not have become obsessive. It was the varying nature of the reinforcement that made us obsessive. Yes, this is what is predicted to occur and yes, this is the underlying dynamic in every abusive relationship.

The power of a consistently neutral response

To get unwanted behavior to stop, you have to remove the reward through neutral response. This will cause the person to start escalating their behavior. If they continue to get a neutral response, they may escalate more, but eventually they will stop.

For instance, had our ice cream in China been just ok, we would never have become obsessive about it. Ok ice cream does not cause extreme responses, in anyone. As silly as this example seems, there really is 70+ years of research to back this up.

Our goal when extinguishing passive-aggressive behavior in the workplace is to remove the reward for the behavior and prevent them from harming the workflow. To do this, we need to consistently remove the reward by providing a neutral response (neither good nor bad) to the passive-aggressive behavior.

When we do this, we should expect them to escalate their behavior for a while before stopping.

With people who do this strategically, they will normally stop when it becomes apparent this strategy is no longer working. For people who are pathological, they will escalate to the point that their aggression is no longer passive. But don't let that scare you. Once the aggression is overt – it is now obvious what is going on and what you need to do to stop it.

~~~~~

CHAPTER 7: HOW TO REMOVE REWARDS FOR A PASSIVE-AGGRESSIVE PERSON

How do you control the dynamic so that a passive-aggressive person is no longer rewarded?

Easy – you work around them and set up systems so that it is impossible for them to restrict information flow and resources. You make it obvious where the bottleneck is. These people are doing this passively, they are hiding their acts of sabotage. Don't let them hide.

The easiest way to do this is to CYA – Cover Your Ass. You do this in a professional, dignified way and with compassion.

Why compassion?

Remember, you do not know at first glance what is really going on or why the work isn't happening. So don't assume you do. Treat everyone with compassion and dignity, and document everything. Your goal is to get clarification. Not to get people in trouble, but in the spirit of figuring out where the bottleneck is, to remove it. Where ever the bottleneck is. This is super important because sometimes, what looks like passive-aggressive behavior, is masking some other problem.

And yes, I do love it when actively acting on my values – like being responsible, compassionate, and professional – is what will most effectively solve the problem.

For Example:

Let me give you an example of how to use CYA documentation to work around a passive- aggressive person AND if it turns out they really are gumming up the works, make it clear to management where the problem really is.

Say you are working with someone and you have a verbal agreement to do something. Send them an email reiterating the agreement and cc their boss and your boss. You do this, not to get them in trouble, but to clarify and make sure that responsibilities are clear. You don't want the confusion of the past to prevent proper problem-solving in the present. You are being professional. This is how professionals solve these sorts of communication problems. They assume everyone is working in good faith and follow-up to try and resolve the communication problem so that the work and problem-solving can occur.

If you don't get the resources they promised, don't get mad. Talk to them. Ask them what happened, and can you do something to help release those resources. They may not be withholding, there may be a legitimate reason they can't get them – maybe someone down their supply chain is withholding or the resources needed just don't exist.

You won't know what the real problem is until you ask. And if they lie, don't worry, that lie will get caught up in the problem-solving. It is not your job to prove they are lying. If they lie, they will get caught in a lie via this process.

Once you have spoken – gotten information on what the problem is – you email again, confirm what they told you, cc the bosses so everyone is on the same page and again, clarify responsibilities so it is clear who is doing what and when to resolve this problem. Give them an opportunity to clarify any misunderstandings you have.

If the resources still don't manifest – repeat. Consistently – every time. Your focus should be on fixing the problem. Not on proving that someone else is a problem. They may be. They may not be. If they are, that will reveal itself to everyone without you having to make the case.

If they aren't a problem – your professionalism, compassion, dignity, and focus on problem-solving – will help make sure the problem is actually solved. Trust me – as emotionally tempting as it is to try and prove your arch nemesis is evil, it won't solve the problem. The only thing that will solve the problem is solving the problem.

When you do this, you will be seen as dignified and professional because you will be. If the other person is not, that will become obvious. You do not need to stoop to their level – ever. Let them wallow if that is their choice. Stay above that and focus on problem-solving professionally and document everything in an effort to provide clarity to the situation.

Here is what happens to truly passive-aggressive people when you do this. They can't hide what they are doing anymore. You are removing the reward because you are preventing them from hiding. They not only can't succeed at stopping or sabotaging the workflow, they will get in trouble if they do.

That's all YOU need to do and that is easily accomplished by excessive CYA documentation. YOU are giving them the benefit of the doubt that they are well-intentioned. If they aren't, they will reveal themselves.

Allowing a Passive-aggressive Person to Reveal Themselves

Here's why. When a reward is removed, the person responds by escalating to get their reward back. If they continue to not get their reward, they will escalate more. Smart strategic people give up quickly. Sabotage isn't as important as not losing their job.

If the person is not being passive-aggressive, and the problem lies elsewhere, they will work with you to fix the problem.

Pathological people, on the other hand, will not be able to help themselves. Their passive aggression will become active aggression. It will be on full display for everyone to see! And again, this is predicted to occur and we have 70 plus years of research to back this up.

If someone is going to blow out spectacularly, there is really nothing you can do to stop them. You really don't need to help them. If they are set on digging a hole they can't get out of, let them. Don't dig it for them. By staying calm, professional, and treating everyone with dignity and with compassion, you can stay above the fray. Focus on problem-solving and leave the stupid interpersonal pettiness to those who can't help themselves.

The Benefits of Being a Dignified Professional

And yes, this not only works, it works great. Remember that passive-aggressive fundraiser? When the board finally moved to fire her, the president of the board called me to let me know that stuff was about to hit the fan and there might be rumors about me, but to not worry because I had the full confidence of the board. He called me before he called the executive director. Professional people recognize and respect other professional people. So be professional, not petty.

This sort of help and respect happens to me all the time. People who respect me do so because I really do try to treat people with compassion and dignity. The bonus is that because I really am focused on problem-solving, they also protect me from aggressive people who try to sabotage me.

I never have to overtly defend myself. I don't think in those terms anyway. When things get bad, I focus on problem-solving. Doing that clears away the clutter and helps me focus on what is important. Good people see that and respond to that positively which is why other people protect me from the nastiness that sometimes is directed at me.

Riding it Out With Dignity

I don't want to give you the impression this is easy. It isn't. When you remove their reward, a passive-aggressive person may become overtly aggressive. When that happens, it can get NASTY.

As a female professional, I have been accused of all sorts of really nasty things, none of which are true. I've not only survived, I survived with my reputation intact and I've held the respect of other people. I survive and thrive because I don't respond to bad situations with bad behavior. I respond with dignity, compassion, and professionalism.

The only time I've lost jobs is when my boss was the problem. Even then, I've never been fired. They have to eliminate my position to justify getting rid of me to top management. That has only happened twice.

Most importantly, I don't have any regrets about how I behaved. Under stress, I behaved consistent with my personal values. I didn't sacrifice my values. Knowing that under stress, I am still a good person is priceless.

~~~~~

38

CHAPTER 8: YOUR GOAL

Your goal is to not let a passive-aggressive individual control the work or information flow. You do this by documenting things professionally with a goal of fixing the problem – not on assigning blame for the problem. Seek to create clarity so that the REAL source of the problem is identified and fixed. Often, the real problem isn't what you think it is. And if it is, then you will be able to act with a clean conscious.

Most importantly, behaving professionally and compassionately while treating everyone with dignity will help reinforce core organizational values and help create a positive work environment. By taking the time to check your assumptions and actually do the work required to clarify what the real problem is, you will not be blaming people who are being sabotaged. You won't accidentally reward a saboteur. Most importantly, you will actually fix your problem.

If there is a workflow problem, focus on fixing the workflow problem. Not on assigning blame. The blame game may feel emotionally satisfying, but it is way more important to figure out how to fix the problem and take responsibility to fix the problem.

This approach eliminates your personal biases and allows you to stay above the fray in what may turn out to be a messy interpersonal matter. You don't have to take sides, you just have to identify the real problem and fix it. And if it turns out there is a person who is actively sabotaging the work of others – get rid of them.

Recap

Passive-aggressive behavior may be a righteous act of resistance, or it may be an active attempt to sabotage work.

By focusing on creating clarity, focused on solving the workflow problem, and treating everyone with dignity and compassion, you can fix your workflow problem ethically and effectively without blaming the people whose work is being sabotaged.

If you do this well, it will help you root out abusive people using passive-aggressive behavior to sabotage the work of others. Focus on fixing the problem. Live your values. Be professional. Succeed.

~~~~~

CHAPTER 9: ABOUT THE AUTHOR

 Jennifer Hancock is a mom, author of several books, and founder of Humanist Learning Systems. Jennifer is unique in that she was raised as a freethinker and is considered one of the top speakers and writers in the world of Humanism today. Her professional background is varied including stints in both the for profit and non-profit sectors. She has served as Director of Volunteer Services for the Los Angeles SPCA, sold international franchise licenses for a biotech firm, was the Manager of Acquisition Group Information for a ½ billion-dollar company and served as the executive director for the Humanists of Florida. When she became a mother, she decided to stay at home, but that didn't last long. Shortly after her son was born, she published her first book, *The Humanist Approach to Happiness: Practical Wisdom*. Her speaking and teaching business coalesced into the founding of Humanist Learning Systems which provides online personal and professional

development training in humanistic business management and science-based harassment training that actually works.

More Learning from Jennifer Hancock

OTHER BOOKS BY JENNIFER HANCOCK

· The Humanist Approach to Happiness

· Jen Hancock's Handy Humanism Handbook

· The Bully Vaccine

· The Humanist Approach to Grief and Grieving

· How to Win Arguments Without Arguing

· Ending Harassment & Retaliation in the Workplace

· Why Bullies Bully & How to Stop Them Using Science

· Reality Based Decision Making for Effective Strategy Development

· Planning for Personal Success

· Why Conflict Management Doesn't Work When the Problem is Bullying

· Why Bullies Bully and How to Stop Them Using Science

· How to Handle Cranky Customer Problems Using Behavioral Science

· How to De-escalate Conflicts Using Behavioral Science

· Bridging the Generation Divide: Millennials vs. Boomers

· How to Talk to Your Child's School About Bullying

COURSES TAUGHT BY JENNIFER HANCOCK
- Workplace Bullying for HR professionals
- Living Made Simpler
- An Introduction to Humanism

- Socratic Jujitsu: How to Win Arguments Without Arguing
- Why Conflict Resolution Doesn't Work When the Problem is Bullying
- Bridging the Generational Divide: Millennials vs. Boomers
- Ending Harassment and Retaliation in the Workplace
- Reality Based Decision Making for Effective Strategy Development
- How to De-escalate Conflicts Using Behavioral Science
- Why is Change so Hard?
- Principles of Humanistic Management
- 7 Sins of Staff Management
- How to Handle Cranky Customer Problems
- New Manager Orientation
- Humanist Group Leadership Lessons
- Sexual harassment training that works – general
- Sexual harassment training that works – AB 1825

- Stop Bullying in our Workplace – Staff Training
- Sexual Harassment Compliance Training
- No Fear Act Training
- Planning for Personal Success!
- Talking to your child about death
- The Bully Vaccine Toolkit
- How to talk to your child's school about bullying
- Why Bullies Bully & How to Stop Them
- How to Prevent Passive-Aggressive People from Wreaking Havoc in the Workplace

CONNECT WITH ME ONLINE:

· **Twitter:** http://twitter.com/#!/JentheHumanist

· Facebook:

http://www.facebook.com/JentheHumanist

· Or sign up for my mailing list:

http://eepurl.com/c3LuI

The End

######